Unmasked

By Shannon McGill

Dedicated
to
Blake, Tyler, Teddy & Achilles

Prologue

Unmasked is a compilation of feelings written through my drastic life changes: worldwide quarantine, falling face first in love, relocating to a familiar safe place, getting that degree, and finding that I can be anywhere and always want growth and change. My roots belong in a specific place that I haven't found yet, and stability for me is growth.

The Pandemic felt special because it was the start of my boys and I being truly alone in a new place. We moved out of the family home and into a whimsical little treehouse with green shutters. We wrote our own songs about the quarantine; I drank too much wine and ate enough charcuterie to transform to a block of boozy expensive cheese . I look back at the videos and see this little trio flanked by our support system and feel so grateful that we had each other to lean into in such a strange phase in our lives. I fell in love hard. I fell in love with the space I shared with my boys and the direction we were headed. I also fell in love with somebody else's son. It felt so good that I can't wait to do it again when I grow up.

I moved to Fayetteville and almost got married.
Those two years were a blur that I wish I could live
again so I could do some things differently, but still
move towards the outcome that led me back to
Oklahoma. Just let me live those two years one more
time in slow motion. I felt a pair of eyes look at me in
a way that destroyed my heart the moment I knew I'd
lost its gaze. Once I realized I couldn't smell his
laundry detergent or cologne anymore, I mourned
my loss hard. I'm not gonna chase the high of that
gaze but I know I'll recognize it when I feel it again.
I know I'm not hard to fall in love with when I'm
being myself; I fall for me every single time like a
dope.
I ever get to fall in love again, the person needs a
desire to protect me as fiercely as I protect myself.
Also, a glove to play catch. Do not approach me
without one.

My dramatic departure and arrival to my hometown landed me in my old neighborhood. I spend mornings before work having coffee with a lifelong friend, I celebrate holidays with people I've known my whole life, and as usual, I fall in and out of love with myself and some people who deserve an eventual apology. Most of my poetry happens from journaling and somehow, I birth another piece about somebody's child who inspired me until they didn't. Being single this time around feels different for me because I'm operating without the indoctrinated need to have a partner.

Do I think children were meant to grow in single parent households? Nah, absolutely not. I never wanted to be divorced, I just am. I hope someone does melt the ice around me. My boys deserve a village; we all do. We need community and each other to grow, so I'm not out here just trying to find a husband or a stepdaddy. I'm building us a whole team that sees us as valuable and worth protecting and uplifting.

The community is here; that's how my books are created. It's in Oklahoma, back in Arkansas, Texas, California. Together we got this degree, we made it back home, and we got this third book. We said we gon' make it, played Jadakiss daily, and we makin' it.

Thank you for surviving this with us. I know it
wouldn't have happened without you.

If there's anything I can say about my life, is that I'm
never in this alone. I may feel like I am sometimes,
but it's never been further from the truth. You might
find yourself in between the lines of these pieces,
it's because I couldn't stop thinking about you.

Contents

Short Stories 56

Haiku

In the Beginning

A relationship haiku

Our honeymoon phase
When we only separate
To fart, burp, and shit

Lies
A fuckboi haiku

Oh, you miss me, huh?
But you leave my texts on read?
See, y'all stay lyin'.

Just Fine

A relationship haiku

Something isn't right
Are you sure, I feel just fine.
You're just fine, I'm not.

Right & Wrong
Another Relationship Haiku

He thinks that he's right
I can't do anything right
It's because you're wrong

I Have a Type

Redhead appreciation haiku

Gingers make me weak
Your freckly face needs sunscreen
Here, let me help you

Strawberries and cream
Rosy skin under freckles
Consent to my grip

Tan, pale, boy, girl, they,
Pixie, Cesar, Locs, Afro
Please hijack my soul!

Poetry & Prose

Embedded in My Roots

That time I tried to write slam poetry.

Fort Hood, Nuremberg, an apartment complex in Tulsa.
Patty's House with the splintery floors, gentrified and out of
my budget three decades later.

A collection of vinyl that still smells like the Army, a pink
ballerina journal with a lock for secrets.

Salem light 100's and $2.00 unleaded, please.

Praying to the setting of the sun wearing a Hijab on Saturdays,
New Jerusalem to ask for forgiveness of our sins on Easter
Sunday.

Clueless and Juice, Wu Tang Clan, NWA and Nirvana,
Malcolm X and Stephen King, Immature and New Kids on the
Block

Center field, a diamond with a well-carved path and a cloud of
dust behind me.

Exclusion, and confusion because my voice was neither "white
nor black."

A family destroyed by drugs, gun violence and grief

A heart that's felt the sting of conditional love enough to
abstain for more

A seed that regenerates itself so that the roots springing from
her body survive in an environment no longer marred by a
history of racism and abuse from its citizens.

Ode to Oui'd

Happy Day that is the same
as any day to my girls and me
We've exercised our freedom to smoke herb
since some of us were brace-faced teens
We rolled our first joint from siblings'
or parents' stash
We stole away to toke outside,
We snuck back in,
Red-eyed, giggly smiled and glad to be alive
Toting $20 worth of QuikTrip snacks,
then crashed.
Before the days of Indicas, Sativas,
percentages and terpenes
there were zero choices
So we got whatever was in the streets
We discovered vast choices of brick weed, brick weed,
And brick weed
Packed tight full of sticks and seeds, sticks and seeds,
Sticks and seeds.
Always coming from some dude too old
to be in the company of girls in their late teens
We said we were old enough
But they always knew
It was to those grown men's favor
that we weren't telling the truth.
So, on 4/20, today, and every day
Tip your spliff to the ladies who legalized
Moved us closer to decriminalize
Because of them we can shop safe
Grow safe and smoke safer indeed
And we don't have to holler at some asshole
to buy shitty brick Oui'd.

mUse

Do you wanna be my muse?
Move me
Inspire me
Ignite me
I'm pointing my finger right at you
Yes, you.
Can I draw my inspiration from your well?
Take this consent to hold my gaze hostage
 like I 'm Narcissus on his knees
Let me use you, muse.
I'll let you muse me, too.

Marriage of Convenience

Grief proposed on the last day of January
Dropped to a knee as I rocked from my hospital bed
Trembling hands stroked my belly
A ring appeared, eclipsing the one on my hand
I accepted, tears streaming down my face,
Eagerly accepting the union that came with an anniversary that
I'd celebrate every year
Happy Birthday, Tyler we love you!
Happy Birthday, Teddy,
I'm killing myself trying not to forget you!
I slipped in an invisible gown
Covered my head in a heavy veil of the same fabric that
mercifully dulled my five senses.
It dissolved my memories and belief of our God
who gives and protects
Because now all I could see and feel
Was everything that ever hurt me, everything I lost
Because it led to this moment,
this last day in January.
It's my very own Battle of Hogwarts,
my own Hiroshima
We always remember our first time
They said I looked mature for my age
I guess that means, I look old enough to handle tragedy
So at the edge of seventeen Grief ripped me open without
consent and held my entire family hostage.
Grief served me nightmares
I swung back at them with cocaine
My nightmares subsided but stole my grounding dreams
I found myself far from my path and just did what I thought I
was supposed to do next.
To escape Grief, I created my own family.

My birth family is now too broken to fix,
let me try my hand at stability.
I held it together, I tried, I promise.
But Grief comes back in a new car
New red haircut, a manicured beard and holds out a hand to say
I'm back, and this time I'm not going anywhere.
I couldn't resist if I wanted to.
My oversized bathtub that provided
weightless safety and comfort
Evolved to a space of suicidal ideation
Closing my eyes, sinking beneath the water
Get me outta here
PLEASE
Let 'em find me floating in my invisible wedding dress that fits
me like a glove
I don't slip out of it and leave it on the floor
Or rip it out like hair extensions
It isolates me and Grief loves it,
I love the validation.
Grief holds my attention while I feel safe.
Eventually, our time together burdens my needs outside of us.
God calls to me through the voices of my people
And I go.
I learn that gown is removable
by my sincere choosing.
The ring kept me from writing,
trapping the thoughts inside my mind.
It comes off and my fingers feverishly release the pain.
I ask Grief:
Do I keep everything because it's temporary
Or let it go for the same reason?
Grief feels like the most reliable being in my life.
I think Grief is where I left him
But he always pops up when I least expect.

Uncle

I'm older than you, like an uncle
Call me Uncle.
You think your big cousins are pretty, don't you?
Do you wanna be like them?
Have a lot of boyfriends?
I can show you how they do it.
Want me to show you?
You don't have straight teeth, a pretty smile
And you are real skinny, too skinny
But you do got ya Mama's booty though
Even though you bony no
You not as pretty but that's okay
Cause I wanna help you.
Come sit closer. Right here on my lap.
Do you like that?
No? You're supposed to.
They like you better if you like it too.
How bout now?
Now?
Stop cryin'
I'm doin' this for your ungrateful ass
See? That's nice, right?
You like it now?
Since you like it, you can't tell.
You wanna be called fass?
If you don't tell nobody, you won't get in trouble.
We can go to the gas station now.
Pick any candy you want.
Go ahead, anything you want.

Towards The End Again

I can tell by my poetry and journal entries
We are about to cycle towards the end
Again.
That happy shit with smiles and giggles
Sighs and cries
Texting with heart eyes
When they start to subside
When you stop greeting me first thing
When you stop greeting me altogether
The poetry that feels so good to create
From being enamored and full of soft dirty words
Twists to prose that makes my loneliness feel desirable
and even romantic
The haikus that convey
In short
The double-edged sword of choosing you
As my Muse
I freefall with my chest bared
Enthusiastically vulnerable to your pain and pleasure
Always unbalanced
Unrequited
 Fierce and unrelenting, desperate even
Inspired when I feel your energy
Ignited when you deny it
It's our song and dance
Always on repeat
I wish you enjoyed playing the part
where you love me
More than when you don't.

Drama Queen

Am I dramatic,
Or are you used to letting people make you
uncomfortable?
Should I stand beside you and be complicit
Suffer alongside you
Misery do love them some company
But Misery doesn't love mine
So y'all say quiet and fester
I'll be the Queen of dramatic un-comfortability
And go without
this undramatically miserable company

Dying Breed

Our daughters will never know what it's like
to be instructed
how to keep
or make a man
anything.
We are the last of a dying breed
Cooking, baking, cleaning for who?
Not us, but you.
Taught by our feminine elders
To be housewives
Keep secret mad money
Water down his booze
Hide physical and emotional bruising
Smile behind the lonely
Because if you're not a wife
You've wasted your entire life.
We are the last of a dying breed
Because now, it's acceptable to just leave.

Submit

You won't break me easy
But I'll damn sure let you try
You might like how I respond
If I catch you handling me
Like something divinely fragile
Breakable
Precious to you
An experience unknown to me
I might like it too much
You won't break me easy
But I'll damn sure let you try

Handful

You're a handful
But you feel too good to release
I take as much of you in as I can before I'm engorged
You're a moving target
I follow you closely with eyes wide open in hopes
that instead of forcing me to chase
or shoot you from midair
Whenever I say
Come 'ere
You float towards my outstretched fingers
Our bodies don't match
We melt together anyways
I said we go together
So, we do.
There's more of you than I've ever experienced,
More than I can fit in both my tiny hands
I clutch what I can and let the rest roam free
I have no problem keeping them full of you
As long as yours stay full of me.

It's Not About You

It's the plans, the fantasies
I prepared for the love of my life
The matching sneakers and outfit combos
The wake, bake, and bed shake sessions
That made us late for work
Holding hands in public
The forehead kisses and soft whispers.
The invisible bubble we erect around each other
when we're in public that makes us feel safe to
recklessly dance and kiss like we're the only people
in the room.
What I want for me will be the same
Whether it's you or somebody else.
So, you see, it's not about you
As usual and always,
It's about me

Energy Vampire

My energy taste good to you?
I'm craved at midnight on a Tuesday
It sounds romantic in theory
But it ain't
You call
I answer and of course,
Validate you
Only you
I 'm exhausted
You're hardly grateful
But you always want more
Me?
I'm fuckin' exhausted.

Turn Around

My arms stay full
my heart pressed against a body
that stopped turning towards me
I lie awake while the snoring vibrates into my skin
Every voice that's rejected me unites
like a Voltron telling me why
I hold you
But you stopped holding me, kissing me good night,
emotionally filling my cup.
I try to imagine what it felt like the last time my own
back felt a heartbeat and I sniff back tears
Not sure why I try to hide it anymore
You don't notice that I'm running out of me to give
until I'm gone.
I told you I didn't feel like myself
I didn't know that there was just none left
Your eyes stare with accusation, disappointment
How can I rely on you?
Where were you?
I was here, behind you,
wishing you'd just turn the fuck around.

Hard Touch, Soft Touch

Ouch, I say.
Hard touch, soft touch, you reply
I never asked for hard touch.
I want to push your boundaries
But I never asked-
Ouch
Hard touch, soft touch, baby
You like this more than me.
I'm just pushing boundaries, baby
But I don't like it
*How am I supposed to know what you like if I don't
push your boundaries?*
Why do you have to hurt me?
*You don't think I would hurt you intentionally, come
on. I can't believe you think I want to hurt you.*
But I was just asking you to stop-
*I would never hurt you intentionally. I'm just
pushing your boundaries. Hard touch, soft touch.
Come on. Finish me off.*
Finish yourself off.

Ungodly

You can't interpret my actions to fit your narrative
A tragedy will never be referred to as
Shannon's Will
Nobody's gonna say
Shannon giveth, Shannon taketh away
or
If the Good Shannon willing
I'm so flawed that
I utilize my heathen behaviors
to fit MY narrative
Sometimes I'm a villain
Sometimes I'm a hero
I'm an Ungodly Goddess
I don't need to forgive all
I'm over here judging you
For mishandling me
I'm over here not forgetting
Planning that somebody out here learns
and doesn't let you repeat your history

The Altar of McConnell

It's never how it looks on TV
it's not always ominous music and dark lighting.
It's not always that shadowy figure in the doorway who
materializes once the house gets quiet
It's "sit on his lap and give him a kiss."
Don't move when his hand slides under your skirt and he
comments on having your mom's ass but somehow bony
it's being reprimanded for trying to hide from the above.
It's a car ride to get candy
It's someone concerned with you, someone who wants you to
know how to please a man
Because every girl should know how to please a man.
It's him telling your cousin to touch you and laughing,
saying, "Look, she likes it!"
It's being called a tattletale and being forced to play alone
because you can't be trusted to keep a secret.
It's participating because they're all you have, and you want to
feel like you belong to someone
anyone, because at age 9 you want to belong
so, you lie and say you like it
you promise not to tell so they will invite you back
You accept gifts for silence
because being ridiculed and ostracized by children and adults-
your own mother- feels worse than what they're doing to you.
You would rather accept what they're doing to you than be
called names and be unwanted.
It's not so bad, everyone else is happy.
Maybe one day I will be too.
At least now, I know how to please a man.

Non-Negotiable

My worth is non-negotiable
Peace is free and never lonely
I ain't playin'
Let's make a deal
How 'bout you
What if you
Why don't you
With none of y'all anymore
What I need the most
You can't afford
And what you're offering
Only benefits you.
A whole me
Is more valuable
To me and mine
Than the large portion of me
That I forfeit for only a sliver of you
Best of luck, you say.
I've never needed luck
Save all that for yourself
That's how you got me over here in the first place

For Us

You can't see her, but she looks just like me
But better
Smarter, stronger, always put together
You'd like her.
She's everything I'm not.
When I'm in a crowd and I'm nervous,
It's not her idea to keep that glass of wine in my
hand
She's not the one afraid of being perceived, but I
can't hear her confidence.
It keeps the hand busy, I reason with her
Since we both like wine
I think
Why not have a sip?
The action of bringing my hand to my mouth
Sipping like the adult I want the world to see
It's comforting until the glass is empty
So out of principle
We get a refill.
For us
I think.

You Like It When I Cry

Look at me when I'm talking to you
I need to watch you hear my words
Releasing them into our atmosphere
while you stare back void of expression
Regurgitation of my insecurities
that are heightened by your behavior
Begging you to tell me how I need to fix me, not you
What do I need to do
to revive the version of you I chose daily
The version of you that reciprocated
You're fine, okay with all this?
But why if I'm crying?
The corners of your eyes crinkle and I see a flutter of
amusement.
Of, course you're happy with how things are-
You like it when I cry

He

Didn't
and Don't
and He probably never will

If
or when
He wants you to remember the good
Remember
He didn't
He don't
and he probably never will

Don't let that distance fool you
He's still what you left behind
Don't let the healing of time
trick you into thinking everything will be fine

We Don't Belong Here

We are bigger, badder
Better
Than Earth
Otherworldly
Magic
Celestial as a muhh-
Shut yo mouf
Godly
I'm in the divine company of a direct descendant of cool
Miles Davis
Nina Simone
Prince
The best parts of Sid Vicious
We make everyone look normal
And they hate it.
Me though?
I'm just tryin to go
wherever it is you go when you leave here
Cause you don't belong
And if not belonging means tasting life through your straw,
spoon, or fork
I'mma follow you right outta here
Ain't even leaving breadcrumbs to find my way back
We can be like Hansel and Gretel
Show me that gingerbread house in the woods
We'll fill up on candy
Act out all the scary parts in the fairy tales
Cause that's us.
We don't belong here
And I love it.

Never Surrender

If I give me to you
Who will I have for me?

Expired Feelings

Feelings should have a smell
So that when the person leaves
the memory is an expired odor.

Sensations from our first perfectly nailed kiss
Suddenly tastes like the morning after a bachelorette
party in your twenties.
The taste of a rolled dollar bill
victim to many suspect noses

We forget the hugs that we wished lasted forever
Do I need to remember how my body warmed from
the inside out when you closed your arms around
me?

I allowed you to melt my armor
because I felt like for the first time, I didn't want it.
I knew when I felt your heartbeat against my chest
It was entirely too close, Shannon.
Too close.

Freeze me again, please.
The world feels,
It feels.
Even worse,
It feels without you

Seasonal Depression

The sun's toasting the gold in my skin
I'm confident and flirty
I want you for the season
We go to bed without clothes on
wake and bake
Play catch, swing a bat, repeat.
I'll do good till mid fall, right before December
Holiday Blues fly in, and I won't be who you
remember
Sad, mean, dismissive and dissociative
melancholy and despondent
devoid of receiving and acknowledging appreciation
Worthless to all mankind
Oblivious to the abusive of myself
Just like Persephone who retreats to Hades
You might need to dip out right now
While I'm still charming and divine
Because by Thanksgiving I'll be the opposite
You don't need to see it, I promise
So, what if we take seasonal sabbatical
And catch-up next Spring
I'll be right back to what you remember,
even better I think
But this way the only one getting hurt will be me.

Grounded

I love the vibration coming from my tippy toes as they lightly
scrape the ground
If my heels touch it feels permanent
and I don't feel like I belong here
Everyone else has chosen their anchor
I glide in brazenly without
In the beginning
I crave the weightlessness of my affliction
The freedom of neither falling nor being carried away
but at times
many regular times
Almost all times
I forget to check for that vibration
and I've left the earth completely
Floating away like a released balloon
Or the wind that keeps everyone else safe
 sends me off my path
My Jordans failing
I fantasize about anchors
I could use one now
One that moves with me
neither pulling nor pushing
guiding gently
regardless of how ungentle I seem
knowing that its good in the beginning
But I'll never disguise
how disrespectfully unavailable I know how to be
when you make me think that you'll choose to let me go

Fraud

Manic happiness controls my ego
The energy temporarily fools everyone in its path
Especially me
I forget and start to skip because I like this person.
I'm happy, capable, desirable, maybe even organized.
For now,
I check to see if anyone is watching me be what I'm supposed to be-
Normal.
It causes me to trip and my baggage hits the ground
Things shatter and I busy myself with picking them up
My fingertips bleed
Significant dates get left behind and forgotten until it's too late
Fear of failure upcoming failure freezes everything
I take on more even though
everything I already have is
Burying me alive
I don't want to look incapable
Yeah, I got it, I'm aight,
Gimme more.
I don't want to disappoint
But I will, and I add your name to the list of people in my mind
who will find out
I'm a fraud
They're gonna find out
that I'm not normal, virtuous, or desirable
When she reveals herself in the mirror
I want to hide.
physically remove her from me
I let you go without a fight
I've been fighting with me forever
I lose every time.

Not Your Baby

I'm not your baby
Before you
I was somebody else's baby
And someone else is now their baby
So, the next person who wants to call me something
anything
Make sure it ain't something
you called everyone before me.

Easter Sunday, 2022
A Journal Entry

I hate Easter.

I always think of my first Easter after the twins were born; I didn't want to do anything, but I had to act like everything was okay when I was still daydreaming of drowning myself in our bathtub. Easter isn't a real holiday to people that don't believe a person can come back to life after three days. I know from experience that if you pray over a dead body for three days; you just watch it change colors.

I found now that I'm hard to handle around Easter because the memory of that first, of me hiding in my in laws bedroom, crying and hitting a vape pen. I'm still that person, crying, hitting a vape pen, physically feeling the pain of a loss that still feels brand new despite everyone and everything around me moving on.

In everything, I'm always last one to let go. I'm afraid of missing the miracle it needs to survive, despite holding death in my arms. I'm reluctant to release the feelings because it may be the last to experience it at its purest.

So today, just like every day for five years I try to be 'normal' while behaving the opposite. Saying I'm okay while doing 'not okay' shit. If it weren't for reflection, I'd be completely unaware; but it doesn't stop it from happening.

Maybe it's the resurrection. Jesus got to wake up. I kept mine for almost 4 days, not in a tomb but in my arms, and that didn't work. All I have left are memories of his skin changing colors and gasping by myself out loud and covering him up, as if the knitted blanket would make it disappear.

Telling the boys' dad that they could take him now, and him coming back to me in a silver urn etched in blue.

To be honest, I forget how I feel about Easter until it comes and I'm emotional, realizing that the werewolf I released was my 'not okay' ripping a giant hole in my 'okay' fallacy.

I'm not okay.
Still

A Million Reasons to Hate Me

You only need one
But I'll give you as many as I want
This is what you get to hate about me.
You're not allowed to choose.

Wanderer

Take your body wherever you please
Your soul though,
That piece stays with me

Dream

Dream with your eyes wide open
You don't want to miss what's next
Even little blinks are a missed opportunity
To exceed the expected

A Real Artist

I wish I was a real artist
I'd pull out my pencil the second you fell asleep
I'd start with your profile, sketching your nose
It's the length of three kisses from brow to tip
And my chin fits perfectly on its bridge
while my lips rest on your forehead
Depending on the week,
I'd shade in the beard you hate growing, but I love
scraping against my bare skin
And marvel at the peaceful smile that parts slightly
to snore during your dreamless sleep
I'd save your hair for last because I know I'd spend
more time touching than drawing
Trying to decide how to capture the feel of silver silk
between my fingers
Your eyelashes should be easy
But they stretch to your cheekbones that carve out
the rest of the masterpiece that is your face
I'm not even gonna try ears.
Ears look hard.
That's the problem with not being a real artist.
I can use a million words
to articulate my favorite view
But I'll never be able to capture you the way I see
you
Perfect.

Seen

Students, locals, jukebox music and dollar drafts
circulated the bar
The heavy smoke thickens the air between us,
making a home in my brand-new weave.
I squint past the smoke, drafts, people, and invisible
music notes
To see him
Leaning against the wall by the ping pong table
Watching me
Watch him
The look in his eyes felt brand new and exciting, full
of romance and desire.
It made me feel seen, chosen, and wanted.
I thought for a second that I was a woman.
We shared tunnel vision, and it was divine.
Then I found myself smiling into a pair of ice blue
eyes now only inches from mine.
He leaned in and whispers to my hair,
"Let's get out of here"
I'd arrived ten minutes before
But I followed him out without a second thought.
The first time I felt someone see me
The sensation traveled through my body and made a
home inside my dreams
Lasting much longer than he wanted
For many years, torturing me.

Bringing me that moment, that night, without words.
We catch each other from across a room full of people
Dream magic places us shoulder to shoulder in a blink
The sensation washes over me
He never suggests we leave
But I follow him through my dream
Blindly and without shame
Knowing that "out of here" will never happen again
Still relishing how the moment felt
I'd wake up feeling guilty and foolish
For reliving something so long ago
It took nearly two decades to realize that the dream wasn't about him
It was about how it felt to be seen.
How it felt for someone to tell me for the first time that I was wanted.

Soft

I crave the feeling of soft,

Squishy and solid, putty in a lap.

Yours or mine? Let's flip a coin

The kind that reacts to warmth and kneading

Needing

The kind that gets pulled into a chest and our
heartbeats sync in time

The kind with heavy sighs and bodies sinking

Melting

Our universes meet and instead of colliding in chaos

It's a harmonic dance of inside jokes and tear-
inducing memories

Whispers purred into your ear in a crowded room
that lead us

'Out of here'

Swollen bottom lips and hands pinning hands

Its as painful as it sounds

Sometimes

But when it's not

Its so, so damn soft

Kingdom of Boymom

Your mama is a jester
Because life is as funny as it is sad
Your mama is a servant
Because you are worthy of being served
Your mama is a knight
Because protecting you is her sworn duty
Your mama is a Queen,
Because all women can choose to rule and be ruled
and your mama rules
Your mama is your mother above all,
Because without you, she's just a silly character
living a fairytale.

Peter Pan

Their kisses taste like honey flavored Peter Pan
I hate peanut butter so much I cringe when I smell it
Residue on the wall in the shape of teeny
fingerprints
Smeared so I know exactly where they've been
And how terrible I'm getting at housework
Noise, clanging, banging, and screaming.
I pause to wait for what comes next
Most times it's a giggle
Other times, it's crying.
Howls of pain vibrate through the floor to my feet,
then straight into my heart.
I don't smell the boys' early lunch
When wet cheeks soak the crook of my neck.
I shower that dirty face with kisses
Our eyes meet and I speak
You're so strong,
You're so brave
I know it hurts now
But it won't all day.
When we chant together
The invisible boo-boo fades into his memories
He's back to himself, good as new.
Without skipping a beat,
Peter Pan climbs back up my nose.
Smeared where he rested on my neck.
I can't stand peanut butter.

I Wish Somebody Would

I wish somebody would fuck with me
I really do
I'm mad, y'all
I really wish somebody would

I chant this to myself as I'm side-stepping toy
excavators
Getting sneezed at while I'm mid-yawn
Wiping an ass that isn't mine
Wiping an ass that is mine
While fingers creep under the bathroom door

Yeah, I really wish somebody would
I been gettin "woulded"
By my own sons
So, if somebody else could

Because I can't do to them
What I would to somebody else
Which is exactly why
They continue to would.
Would someone else,
Please?

Tiny Apple, Giant Tree

I tell you NO

Eyes almost identical to mine glare back at me
defiance

Barely three feet above the floor.

My mother and her mother's temper makes me want
to knock you to the ground

My memory of getting up from the ground changes
my mind

My older brother's face squeezes in rage as tears
flow and you eat the snot running from your nose

"That's not food" I remind you

But a flashback reminds me that I, too, once thought
boogers were food.

In my baby brother's fashion, your cries turn to
giggles and your mouth spreads across your face

Just like your daddy, you forgive almost instantly

Just like me, I can tell you don't forget.

Bupropion, Wellbutrin, and Gabapentin

An invisible fist sucker-punches me in the gut

I don't even flinch

A lump inflates inside me like a swallowed watermelon seed

My feet stay planted, and my expression is impassive

I should be very fucked up over this, I know.

My eyebrows furrow in confusion as my chest tightens

The lump inflates, applying pressure on my throat

I imagine vines spilling from my mouth, nose, and ears as my
eyes start to itch, threating to do something.

I think I'm supposed to cry.

Yes, I'm supposed to cry, I *want* to cry

Tears create a window that blinds me
and I blink to force them out.

Nothing comes, I stand still.

holding my breath while I wait for myself to feel.

Middle Child, Cusp Capricorn

Between two brothers
The end and beginning
Beginning and the end
Contradicting needs and unwavering
inconsistencies
Demanding quiet and controlled chaos
Simple complexity
Everything needs consequences
Everything but me
I am the exception
Exc-ep-tion-all-y

Rejection

We appreciate your submission

But

Words and words, your submission was not chosen.

I tear apart each sentence every other hour

Just in case there's something I missed

A small clue between the appreciate and the rejection

That says something

Anything

Except that I'm not chosen.

It's worse than a break-up text

Say you like someone else,

My best friend, your ex,

Even say you don't like me

Just don't start your message with

Good afternoon

We appreciate your submission,

But

Wet Dream

You stir me awake
I still feel your big spoon
breathing desire into my small
Your elbow bends
Fingers spider-crawl from my chest to my
collarbone
Resting to lightly circle the base of my neck
A sensation so intense that it out outshines the
butterflies in my stomach seizes my whole body.
I'm yours, and you treat me like I shouldn't expect
any more or less than what's already there.
I grip your hand and apply pressure while my hips
move at your command
I wait to hear you sigh into my ear, say my name.
Gasping in anticipation
Silence
You're not a remarkable lover
You're just a guilt seizing, unreliable, captivating
Dream

Moon Salutation

My chin tilts up
Her beams spill down the tip of my nose
Tracing my cheekbones, resting on my shoulder
blades
I worship Her through every divine phase
I wane with Her wax
I wax with Her wane

Crusaded

My first religious act of violence
came in the form of a threat
If you commit sin, You Is Damned to Hell.
"If" implied that sin was avoidable
As soon as I learned to read, it horrified me to find
that within the pages of this reproduced pile of
literature
The threat wasn't 'if,' it was 'when.'
I'm always going to mess up, I should always feel
shame, I will be judged, punished, and unlovable for
an amount of time by elders, and depending on the
sinner's likeability, their sins are overlooked.
Even the bad ones, especially the bad ones.
If you're the most liked in your community, your
sins are accepted.
But not 'when'
Only 'if'
I knew before I was a teenager that I would never be
liked enough to sin like the men I knew
Like my parents, my brothers even.
In a book of blanketed and arbitrary sins built to
sustain years of feudalism and caste systems,
the possibilities of damnation to are endless
Especially as a woman
All documented historical evolutions in religion are
traced

by the lives it took, the spaces it consumed, it's
colonization
Rather than their divine miracles
Victims fall long before their 'when'
No one admits that we choose the 'when,' not God
To belong to something bigger than you that isn't
tangible
Requires submission of critical autonomy
Submission of empathy past indoctrination which
for some is surprisingly simple
The rest of us ask questions and feel confused by the
answers
I listen quietly for the voice that's supposed to tell
you what to do in prayer
Beg and bargain with whatever we were told is
floating above us
I hear myself providing the encouragement, my
voice telling me to keep going
But the threats, the judgment, the shame
Those are religious voices trying to hold me captive
from myself
When people judge and decide based on what God
says I ask myself
Is this what they think He said, or what they wish he
would say?
Are you deciding on 'if' you hear Him, or 'when'
you heard him?

Short Stories

White Diamonds

Her voice wakes me up at six am, "Time for school."
She leaves for work minutes later, and the scent of
White Diamonds left behind in her wake acts as the
snooze button pulling me from the wooden bunk
bed I shared with overnight guests or my younger
brother.

Her voice is the intercom inside me that seems to
know the urgency that I need to be to school in time
for the bell, despite her being in her Altima driving
up Highway 75 to her job at Pepsi. I've left the bed
and took to lying on the floor above the vent,
allowing the hot air to puff up the top sheet I draped
over me, creating a heated tent around me.

I can't see a clock, in fact there isn't one in my
bedroom but my sleepy eyes blink open when I hear
her announce, just as she'd done before leaving
home to work, "TEN MINUTES!"

I leave the sheet on the floor because I don't hear
her telling me to put it away and stomp towards the
bathroom so Googie can hear me moving
downstairs. He's much harder to wake, especially
since Vaun left.

In the bathroom I almost always get lost in the vanity
mirror that stretches horizontally across the
bathroom wall. My new braids keep me from having
too much to do in preparation for school, and I smile
at my reflection, showing off the braces I begged her
for. "Grease your scalp," the intercom purrs."
Don't forget behind your ears. You're so pretty.
The prettiest girl in your whole school."

I frown at my pretend conversation with Mama. I
might be, could be, if I wasn't black. If. I looked like
the others, maybe.

She replies, but this time sounding like her mother,
Grandma Allie. "It's because you're black, because
you're you, that you're prettiest girl in your whole
school. No one will ever look like you, but they will
stare into the sun to mimic the shade of your skin,
but you wake up with it every morning."

I know they're telling the truth because they're the
most beautiful women I've ever known but because
I'm only sixteen I feel like it's different for me,
because I'm not them. I study my face and find that
I'm not displeased with what I see, I'm displeased
with what my peers don't see.

Yes, I AM beautiful. My eyes don't need mascara, but I'll use just a little, and since Mama can't catch me, I'll even wear the lipstick I stole from the mall. Why did I steal it anyway, I ask myself? Because Mama said you couldn't buy lipstick… Well but isn't it more trouble if—

"FIVE MINUTES!" White Diamonds invades my nostrils from the hallway, and I rush out of the bathroom, ignoring Mama's call to finish my edges.

Flower Mound Road

In early 2001, my older brother relocated from his room downstairs to a prison cell in Lawton, Oklahoma on Flower Mound Road, in the middle of nowhere. The first Christmas he lived there, we piled into Daddy's Maxima and took the four-hour drive to Lawton.

We all liked the same music, so nobody wore headphones; it's one of the best parts of my family. Wherever we went, car rides were fun. We always sang together, talked, played games. There was your typical back seat brawl that got the car pulled over and everybody's ass beat, but for the most part our chemistry as a family was magical. Everybody was funny, we had so many inside jokes, and we loved each other's company.

No one was looking forward to this trip so Goog and I woke up early and rolled a blunt before anyone could go downstairs. We used to get up early to open presents, but this year Christmas was in the back of our minds, to the point that I spent my first of many years after decorating the tree alone. This trip would also mark the year that I officially loathed my birthday, December 22nd. The year I turned eighteen I spent my Christmas driving to a prison, in brand new jeans, a pair of platform boots, and a sweater I'd picked out in Old Navy three days before. This was the first year I kept half the things we bought that day, and the other half went under the tree. Merry Birthmas, Shannon. Paying for Vaun's defense made Christmas and my birthday a lot less elaborate for me, and I was a spoiled teenage girl, so I was pretty pissed off about it. I kept a personal list of things in my head, and this was filed under, Things about Vaun's Murder that Make Me Mad. Under that list were witnessing my baby brother's panic attacks and hearing my mother wail from her bedroom every night.

Daddy printed out the directions on Mapquest and used the most primitive of GPS devices. For over two hundred miles we drove on I-44, everyone cycling from joking to crying, then painful silence as we got closer to the prison, then called Wackenhut Correctional Facility. Goog and I giggled out of nervousness and sang along to Three-Six-Mafia from the back seat. My parents didn't make a sound.

An abandoned radio station sat on the road, and I wondered when it was last inhabited and what music was played. This tiny square building; can't remember the name of the station. You could tell by looking that it was a dead space, bugs probably didn't even mess around in there. Even the snow surrounding the building looked dilapidated and forlorn. Later in life the station would take the vision of an abandoned building in one of Stephen King's *Bizarre of Bad Dreams.*

Flower Mound Road is a long, flat stretch, surrounded by farmland. Signs along the side of the road warn against picking up hitchhikers. I told myself that if my brother were hitchhiking, I'd pick him up. Nobody else, though. My Aunt Terri told me a story about hitch hiking that let me know a lot of the women in our family are lucky to be alive. It also gave me the idea that I might be as protected as the McConnell women who to me, stared down all danger with fists at their sides.

When you're a teenager full of imagination, you imagine a prison the way you see it in Disney movies, a dungeon. Dark corners with rats scurrying everywhere. Maybe a few ghosts, but most definitely, bars and concrete everywhere. Cobwebs in every single corner. A magician disguised as an old man who leads you out through a secret passage.

It's not like on television; inmates are separated from visitors until you go the visiting area. The visitors' area is an open room full of chairs. People from all walks of life crowd in these lined chairs and nobody really looks that excited to be there. A woman who I think showed up in the expensive Kompressor gets sent outside with instructions to leave her Louis Vuitton bag in the trunk and only bring in her ID and keys. Her eyes are red-rimmed as she passes us to the front door. I wonder who she's there to see. A small Cherokee girl with missing fingernails sits in front of me; turned around to face me. I make a few faces, and she turns back around. We play the game until our names are called over the intercom and we line up to be searched.

You take off your shoes and socks, and they swab our hands, searching for contraband. I receive my first of many frisks and I open my hands for her to swab. The swab turns a weird color and I cock my head to the side.

"What does that mean, ma'am?"

Her eyebrows furrow, and she says, "Probably nothing. Go ahead, you're good, sweetie."

"Thanks. Merry Christmas, ma'am." Then I
remembered that I forgot to wash my hands after
rolling and smoking that blunt. Whoops. We put
our shoes back on and begin our trek towards Vaun,
who we hadn't seen in months.

Concrete and fences are everywhere, I was right
about one thing. The campus, which is what they call
it, is separated into many little pieces that connect
by straight pathways with fences on either side. It's a
campus now, and not a prison. Every hundred feet
or so, a gate separates you from another fenced in
hallway- you gotta wait until someone buzzes you in
at each gate.

EEHHHHHH
EEHHHHH

It swings open and you head to another fenced
hallway and repeat the process until you reach
another building, one that looks like a school
cafeteria.

Campus.

From there you're directed to a little numbered
table where your person is either seated, or you wait
until they arrive.

Anxiety floats at the ceiling so you breathe it in and exhale for the person across from you to share. We are all high from the anxiety fumes, each table. Men in navy blue jumpsuits stare across to a mother, father, sibling, or lover at their table while snacking on food from the vending machines that lined a side wall.

Vaun loves the burgers, M&M's, and soda. We make sure to bring at least $20 in quarters, to give him whatever he wants, and he always offers it to us. I know he wants to share, like a normal family visit but I want him to eat it all because I can eat that shit anytime. I want him to enjoy it but if I took note, he would enjoy it more if we ate together.

For a couple hours I'm in the cafeteria with him, fighting tears and laughing, getting annoyed or angry. I feel it all in that time together.

Goog and I sit with our arms crossed. Everyone cries when we see him approach us in his jumpsuit. This is where he lives now. My brother lives in here with all these criminals. My brother isn't like these guys. He shouldn't be here.

Yeah, he should, a voice chimes in my head. This voice is angry with him. This voice sees the trip, the plethora of life inconveniences, the shame of having a murderer in the family, and the nightmares of prison rapes as a reason to be angry. The voice blames him for everything.

Meanwhile, he's smiling and talking like everything will be okay. I feel this strange connection to many of my dreams already in my young age, so I wonder if the things I saw in my sleep ever happened to him. I try to see if something about him looks different. I don't speak, I just watch everything.

I don't remember what we talked about; I tried to memorize the room. I wanted to find similarities in the people there. I wondered if the families were like us, normal until that one day. Everything was okay, kinda normal. Every family has its problems, right?

Surely one of the families in this room got dealt a shitty hand just like us. One thing I know eighteen years later is that those guys in the room were lucky to have visitors. Whether the guy was a good kid who made a mistake or a hard-core criminal, he was lucky to have visitors.

Most of those guys in there don't hear from family or friends until they get out; sometimes never again.

I wish I could say visits got easier after that, but I'd be lying. The time I took in between visits was due to the shame of not coming sooner. It was also because I feared coming to visit and finding his face bruised, eyes black from an attack like my nightmares.

I had such a clear vision because he'd been in a fight in David L Moss. I was so traumatized that the only thing I remembered from that visit was his face. I never wanted to see it like that again.

I think I've visited my brother about five or six times by myself and haven't since my thirties. I'm usually fine on the highway, it's just Flower Mound Road. Butterflies appear in my tummy and flutter for the entire time I'm there. I try to remind myself that he isn't going to look like he does in my dreams, twenty-one years old. Every time I see him is a shock because he's aged. Where did Vaun go? Who is this grown ass man? Where is my brother?

"How's Goog?"

"I don't know, the same," I shrug. "If he's doin' wrong, we won't know where he's at; right now, he's safe at home, so I guess he's okay. "

I feel like we have the same conversation when we
bring up our baby brother. He blames himself; want
it, I want you
And even though we both know I'm cooler
I'm afraid I won't impress you
I blame him too.

"When I get out, everything will be better. I can
help him."

Me, the eternal optimist who believes I will always
escape danger, trouble, or tragedy in the end,
decides not to respond. I never respond when he
talks like that, planning his eventual return to our
family. The family daydreamer can't conjure such a
thing.

I look away and try to think of something else to say,
because when he talks about coming home, I feel
angry. You can feel the resolve in his voice, the
confidence that if given another chance he can help.
He can fix it all.

One of the things we have in common.

I wonder if people feel like this when I romanticize
an idea or plan, they think is impossible.

I feel so uncomfortable, so sad. So frustrated.

He's my older brother, yet I feel like I need to protect him and his feelings now. I don't know how to fix this, so I get more anxious and start checking the clock on the wall to leave. You don't wanna be that asshole who leaves early, he's all you get to see until someone else decides to come. And no one ever comes.

The room isn't even full of people on visiting day; tables are empty, and I imagine the other men who don't have visitors, those who became out of sight and out of mind.

I know that's happened to Vaun; I know because I've done it myself. I feel so guilty that it makes visiting him hard. I know I should and can do better, but he is the easiest and most painful part of my life to avoid.

I can't hate myself for it because regardless of the importance of forgiveness, I know the day that brought him here never should have happened.

After the Dust Settles

I just wanna know which person thought it was
noble to silently suffer the feelings that are left over
after you separate from someone.

How do you reconcile the feeling of an inside joke
you can't share anymore, or a conversation you can
never rehash?

Who talks about the memories of when everything is
just perfect, and you touch each other every time
you pass?

Now you walk through the empty kitchen
remembering a time when someone would wrap
their arms around your waist while you're watching
the bacon.

You forget the loneliness that came after those
months of feeling whole.

I felt whole with him longer than I didn't, but I could
tell waiting for it to circle back would be fruitless.

I wanted him to be sad, at least a fraction of how sad
I feel.

I don't want to think that I'm the only one who
remembers.

The dust has settled and all that's left of me in your
place are the bobby pins and leftover strands of hair
that haven't been picked up by your Roomba.

Once I couldn't feel you hurting me and the pain
subsided

All I can think about now is how good we felt, before
we didn't

How good it felt to watch you see me

To smile when you saw me, pull me into your arms

When the hugs lasted longer than our attention to
whatever was on Netflix

When you opened the door for me every time I came
home

When you'd guide me to our bedroom while you
kissed me,

When I faked being a 5am coffee drinker just so I
could watch the sun rise with us

I ask myself now if you would have chosen me if I
hadn't gone back to sleeping in

If I had met the expectations, I never knew I missed

If I didn't let me destroy myself to someone you
didn't recognize and had to now fend off

I'm so sad.

I know it won't last forever if I don't let it

But right now, I hurt, and I mourn the feelings you
gave me before they were lost on us

I feel foolish looking back and wanting that.

Wanting that spark that made me run blindly to you

That spark that made you take a two-hour commute
almost every day

I ask myself when it went wrong.
I almost think I know, but I can't say I'd change
anything.

Nightingale Pledge

Before God and those assembled here, I solemnly pledge;
To adhere to the code of ethics of the nursing profession;
To co-operate faithfully with the other members of the nursing team and to carry out faithfully and to the best of my ability the instructions of the physician or the nurse who may be assigned to supervise my work; I will not do anything evil or malicious and I will not knowingly give any harmful drug or assist in malpractice. I will not reveal any confidential information that may come to my knowledge in the course of my work. And I pledge myself to do all in my power to raise the standards and prestige of the practical nursing; May my life be devoted to service and to the high ideals of the nursing profession.

-Nightingale Pledge, modernized.

A fly on the wall or invisible spy in the intentionally darkened office at Saint Crystal's Regional Hospital would immediately assume that Head Nurse Shannon Ashley wasted her mornings doom scrolling social media from her desk. Dark curls streaked with subtle glimmers of silver rioted from her scalp and tumbled to her shoulders softly. She held a handful of thick tendrils in her free hand, twirling absently. Her brow furrowed over narrowed hazel eyes as she collected a screen shot from her iPhone, sighed in disgust, and crossed another name off the mile long list of candidates.

She could smell and taste her breakfast smoothie from under her medical grade mask and removed it, relishing the quick break from masking. She'd been at the hospital since six that morning, reviewing the list of nursing candidates to invite to their overflowing hospital. Since the Pandemic, St. Crissy's lost a large percentage of its staff to COVID diagnosis, fear of diagnosis, and refusal to vaccinate. The remaining nurses were averaging 70-hour weeks and the stress beat them mercilessly.

She'd been at the search for weeks, but she knew that no one else cared enough to be this thorough. Her needle in the haystack might be a myth in their little community. She hoped not, she herself was a needle, she reasoned. The sharpest needle there.

I'mma poke all these motherfuckers, she thought to herself with a dry laugh. Her phone dinged, and a banner notification said that she had meetings in twenty minutes. She only had twenty minutes left.

"Twyla James, R.N.," she repeated the name with an exaggerated drawl cultivated from a culturally colorful upbringing in the South. She grew up poor, the only white girl in her black neighborhood. She graduated high school and partied through college, barely making her Bachelors. That felt like a million years ago, but she still felt the same pride as she glanced at the photo of her, her family and best friends at her pinning ceremony. Over twenty years ago she pledged the same promise every nurse in her hospital made in their own ceremonies and she couldn't help but wonder if anyone else heard those words.

She entered the name in the search engine from her desktop computer and a list of social media accounts under that name populated the screen. The name was common, Twyla James. She could be this Black woman holding a pair of chubby adorable twins. Maybe the Twyla James with the nose ring and crop top. Shannon decided to begin her search with Black Twyla with the babies. She hoped this Twyla could be her needle.

She was not. This Twyla wasn't even a nurse; she appeared to be a church pastor. On to Nose ring Twyla.

She pressed her thumb over the picture, pulling up Nose ring Twyla's social media. She gazed up at Shannon Ashley, lips puckered, fingers up in a peace sign, puppy ears wagging. She started by looking at her profile pictures, selfies mostly of her making the same face with a different filter sporting another animal's ears. Twyla as a kitten, bunny rabbit, devil horns. Twyla as a sparkly person with aviator glasses. Twyla liked Snapchat.

She also was not her needle. On to another Twyla.

Her thumb swiped over her profile section. Twyla's birthday was in January. Relationship Status: Married. Anniversary, August 4. A masked picture of her in scrubs graced her profile picture.

Please God, let this be my needle.

Her timeline looked interesting, active. Graphics with positive, affirming quotes about self-love and women empowering others. Shannon Ashley giggled as she landed on a picture of Twyla and a group of women posing with their wine glasses held high, toasting an event. They looked drunk and excited to be alive. Twyla liked to party. She kept scrolling. She liked this Twyla so far.

About a week into the timeline, Shannon Ashley
stops. She found exactly what she was looking for, her
turd in the punchbowl. She took her screenshot, placed
a red line through Twyla James, and checked the next
name on her list. Lawrence Wright. She entered his
name in the search engine and was surprised to see that
he played college basketball at a west coast college. He
owned profiles on every social media app but appeared
to share very little about himself. Single, no children.
No political views.

Promising.

Unfortunately, and quickly, Lawrence also failed her
test. She took the screen shot and sent it to her
roommate.
"Look, a nurse in a Rebel Flag bikini," she texted,
dropping the eyeroll emoji.

"The South will rise again, Massa," Karin replied,
adding a laughing emoji "How can you expect a
Daughter of the Confederacy to care for a diverse
population?"

"You don't," Replied Shannon Ashley. She dropped
her phone into the pocket of her scrubs and tossed her
hair. She looked at the Nightingale Pledge framed on
her wall and read it softy, reminding herself that in her
hospital, everyone would be taken care of, regardless of
who they were.

She finished her pledge and adjusted the Black Lives
Matter mask over her medical grade. She thought about
the LPN she fired two weeks ago for calling a
Venezuelan patient an 'illegal.' She recalled the
surgeon who couldn't keep his hands off her, finally
gone after a lengthy and reluctant battle from HR.
Somebody had to keep the wolves out.

You're the needle in the haystack, Shannon.
She feels her phone vibrate and looks at the screen.

"Poke those motherfuckers," Karin's text said, adding
a needle, string, and a flexed arm.

"Duh, bitch," Shannon Ashley replied, dropping her
phone back into her pocket as she shut the door.

Shannon McGill rarely takes no for an answer
and founded Get Write to publish her own work.
Her mission is to help writers publish on their own
terms and share their stories with the world. She's
been performing poetry since her teenage years and
as a mother to three boys in the beginning of her
forties, Shannon finds more stories to tell that
remind the world that life is so funny that it's sad,
they're not alone, and at least there's always a light
to be shed in the darkest spaces.